THROUGH
ONE
MAN'S
EYE

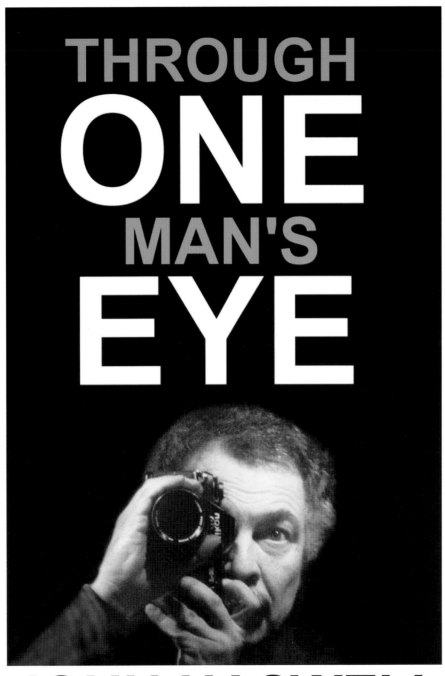

JOHN HASWELL

THROUGH ONE MAN'S EYE
The personal story of travelling with a camera

JOHN HASWELL

Titles and text editing : Sheila and Derek Wagg
Design and photographic selection : David Haswell

Gavenny Graphics

A Gavenny Graphics Publication
First published in 2004 by Gavenny Graphics
a Subsidiary of the Gavenny Press
Invergowrie, Windsor Road, Abergavenny
Gwent,Wales, UK. NP7 7BB
01873 850440

A catalogue record of this book is available from the
British Library

ISBN 0-9547652-0-6

Titles and Text Editing: Sheila and Derek Wagg
Book Design and photographic selection: David Haswell

Typesetting by MRM Graphics Ltd
Printed and bound by Kyodo Printing Co, Singapore
under the supervision of MRM Graphics Ltd, Winslow,
Buckinghamshire, UK

Gavenny Graphics extends special thanks to: David, Pip and
Toril Brancher, Mark Dutton, John Bartlett, John Geraghty,
Larry Thomas, Agnese Geldard, Umar Hussain,
Janet and Gordon Davies

CONTENTS

Introduction	8-9
Prologue	10-11
Kenya	12-27
Egypt and Turkey	28-37
Pakistan	38-49
China	50-63
Vietnam	64-71
India	72-101
Ecuador	102-113
Russia	114-125
Morocco and Algeria	126-143
Italy	144-165
Epilogue	166-173

Introduction

John Haswell was born on 21st July 1947 of an Anglo-Italian family in Ferryhill, County Durham. He was educated at St. Joseph's College, Dumfries, and the University of Edinburgh, where he qualified as a civil engineer. After a period with MacAlpine and Ove Arup and Partners, he went on to become chief estimator with Wimpey Environmental, the geo-technic contractors.

Influenced by his uncle, Frank Cocozza, his interest in photography was evident in the very early years. As a student with limited funds, he shared his equipment and many photographic trips with his brother David. David gives an account of one journey in particular, when the teenage pair arrived in Venice with very little money – enough to pay for three nights on a campsite, a decent meal or a roll of film. They settled for a discreet and unofficial tenting pitch in an orchard and bought the film.

Fortified by a diet of unripe fruit and Andrews Liver Salts, they set about the serious task of planning 36 carefully calculated camera shots. This had more to do with location than sun angles, for the exercise was undertaken beneath cloudy skies and Venetian drizzle, this being a year of record floods in northern Italy. Rewarded with sunshine on the third day, they undertook the shoot, alternating each frame to an agreed plan, rivals in the competition for best picture. The journey home was achieved with a rucksack full of fruit and the help of a pre-paid rail ticket. For John this was to be the first of many trips to Venice, capturing reflections of light, boats and buildings in his photographic imagery.

In a small way the Venetian trip was typical of John's approach to his lifetime hobby. He was prepared to travel great distances to off-beat locations to capture the mood of a country and its people. He did so alone, often straying into territory forbidden to westerners. He confessed to being equally excited and terrified by the risks he was exposed to as a lone traveller in Vietnam, the North West Frontier and South America. On several occasions he would be let down by the shortcomings of a long distance taxi driver, the inadequacy of translation in his travel documents or the weakness of his lower back. Often his adventures ended with a trip to the osteopath or hospital on his return home. Twice, when suffering from back pain, he traded his spare camera to pay for a more comfortable mode of transport from hotel to airport.

John died in August 1998, aged 51, at the commencement of a trip to Burma. At our last meeting with him we gave warnings of the risks involved, but to no avail; the tickets for the journey were already in his possesssion, and he had made up his mind to make this his next photographic adventure. We wished him well and arranged to meet on his return to Edinburgh. He may have had a premonition of his untimely death, because his last words to us were a reminder of a promise we had made some time previously to publish, should any misfortune befall him, a book containing a selection of his best photographs. These words took on a new significance in the light of the subsequent tragic events, and we have tried to honour his wishes to the best of our ability.

When early reports of John's death filtered through, it was wrongly assumed that he had been a victim of local circumstances, such were the challenges likely to be encountered by foreign travellers. In fact he died of a heart attack, probably brought about by deep vein thrombosis, within hours of reaching his hotel close to a Buddhist monastery on the outskirts of Bangkok. According to his diary, the plan had been to visit the monastery the following day to complete a series of photographs of the Thai monks he had begun on an earlier trip. He made no secret of his fearful and intense dislike of flying, and only used this hated mode of transport as a necessary evil to cover great distances in the shortest possible time.

John was constantly seeking perfection in his camera shots, and, whenever conditions permitted, would photograph the same subject many times over until he had achieved what he considered to be a satisfactory result. On several occasions, however, his quest for perfection prevented him from seizing the first opportunity of photographing the very subjects which he had travelled so far to see; he may have been waiting for better weather or more attractive background features before committing the images to film, but this cautious approach often cost him dearly and he missed several golden opportunities which never came his way again. This was noticeably the case when he had only a short holiday at his disposal and time was of the essence.

Despite this somewhat inexplicable habit of procrastination, John still contrived to amass over 24,000 photographs from his travels. His brother David undertook the daunting task of choosing the best of them for this volume. John also compiled rough notes on several, although not all, of his journeys, written in his own inimitable hand, undoubtedly artistic but not always easy to decipher. The manuscript is peppered with gaps, squiggles and question marks, where the author was either at a loss for words to express the emotion of the occasion described, or (more likely) intending to "look it up at home", where he had access to travel books and detailed maps, from which he could obtain accurate distances between places visited and the correct spellings of unfamiliar foreign locations. In his busy working life there was seldom enough free time available for him to fill in these gaps when he returned home, but the editors have attempted to do their best with the material he left behind to provide a sympathetic rendering

Into the Light

I cannot exactly recall when I took my first photograph with any serious intent. What I do remember well was the realisation that photography is a wonderful method of satisfying the artistic urge within someone of precious little natural patience. Experience has also shown me that photography, at

Into the Light

PROLOGUE

1

Meeting the wildlife and people of the Masai Mara

KENYA

KENYA

Kenya

Meeting the wild life and people of the Masai Mara

By 1991 I had been travelling with a camera for some ten years or so, but during that period, because people and landscapes had up until then absorbed my interest, I had never undertaken a planned trip with Natural History for my subject. However, during that particular year I recall feeling for the first time that my camera work had suffered a certain imbalance, and that Natural History had certainly been placed on a back-burner. I was also beginning to take an increasing interest in the work done by Edinburgh's Zoological Society.

Whilst Edinburgh strives, in the main successfully, to respect its animals and to place them in sympathetic habitats, there is no doubt in my mind that such creatures are best photographed within their own natural environment; and therefore in Summer 1991 this meant going to either Kenya's Masai Mara or the Serengeti of Tanzania. An obvious advantage to the photographer was, of course, the possibility of finding an endless variety of secondary elements to a composition – a dramatic sunrise or a gentle sunset, the wonderfully architectural acacia trees, not to mention interesting low-level eye to eye confrontations through the long grass with the local wildlife. As an extension of the primary purpose of the visit, to photograph the Natural History of just a tiny corner of this vast continent, I would also have the chance of meeting the local population. And so, having finally settled on Kenya's Masai Mara and agreed a basic itinerary, I looked forward with great anticipation to my trip.

Flying via Cairo, and surviving a mid-air fire on board the plane over Alexandria, I joined a group of some dozen people, assembled from all parts of the globe, in a down-town Nairobi tourist office. If the in-flight entertainment caused concern, it proved to be a minor technicality compared to sharing my first African night under canvas with a herd of boisterous hippos who had emerged from the waters of Lake Baringo. At nightfall, a campsite official had passed around a litany of "Do's and don'ts" in the event of receiving such a family visit; but truth to tell, all present without exception had not taken the warnings very seriously and suspected that the official was playing a practical joke on the company. The ensuing nocturnal happenings soon disabused us of this unworthy thought and we spent an interesting, informative but sleepless night in repentance. A subsequent visit upshore to the Leakey Snake Farm at Baringo proved child's play in comparison with our first-night experience at the campsite, and we were relieved to find that these initial nerve-shattering events would not be repeated too often during our stay.

Around the mid Kenyan lakes, larger sized water-birds were my intended quarry, and in time we were to meet each other on the eastern shores of Lake Nakuru. Pink flamingos, pelicans and the odd fish eagle were grouped warily around the water's edge. To have a really intimate encounter with these birds, a wide silty foreshore had to be traversed, and having travelled some thousand miles to do business with them I came to realise that these shores, 80 metres wide, were sown with Kenya's own variety of anti-personnel traps in the shape of dozens of wart hogs, all darting about hither and thither. At first glance it appeared that such small compact buzz-bomb creatures could not possibly pose any real threat to anything larger than themselves; however, very soon afterwards I witnessed their unprovoked terrorising of a group of water-buck; and later, when I saw one of them attacking as fair game the rear axle of a Landrover, I concluded that I had a problem on my hands.

After half an hour of deliberation I was almost ready to assume the rôle of war-photographer, although I still had reservations about the safety aspect. Then two things happened to change the situation, immediately and for the better. A sudden unexpected downpour occurred, resulting in the hogs moving landward towards the less exposed wooded shores of the lake, and our driver Peter decided to accept my token gift of 30 Kenyan Shillings to ferry me half-way across the width of the foreshore in his transit van. In the happy expectation that nothing more could possibly happen to thwart my plans, I proceeded at a rapid pace with the photography. How graceful the birds were in flight – and how ridiculously ungainly when landing! Again, how magnificent the flamingos looked when following their leader, describing cyclic flight patterns – a truly spiritual experience, no doubt about it.

Eventually, after passing through the Lake Naivasha area, we reached the Masai Mara Game Reserve. The August evening cast its saturated ochre hues far and wide across the valley, pin-pointing individual wildebeest that had broken away from the clustered groups numbering tens of thousands – a chain in perpetual, apparently blind motion. Looking to the west and north-west, I tried to decide which available groupings might form the basis of a panoramic sunset, now almost ready to burn out; I hoped that all on board would wish to share the experience, if not the photographic opportunity. The time had come to make Peter aware of my intentions but unfortunately he had other plans, namely to get to our camp without delay. Sadly, the opportunity for a genuinely good photograph remained unfulfilled, never to be repeated during our four-day excursion in the Mara. On occasions like this I am obsessed with the idea that the best photographs are unquestionably those that are missed; the mind, almost through spite, insinuating that the lost photo-opportunity would have undoubtedly produced a masterpiece.

If Kenya's wildlife had conspired to defeat my objectives, not so the pictorial treasures offered by the sight of the Mara's people, passing with their cattle daily through our tented village on the banks of the Talek river. It was a glorious location, situated on the eastern margins of the Mara, the river acting as a kind of moat between the nightly bellows of the Mara's animal inhabitants and the ever watchful dwellers of the tented village, who should have been sleeping but were not. Early morning tranquillity (induced no doubt in part by the reassurance of yet another night survived in those parts) would be brought to an immediate close with the tinkling of bells – not the Angelus calling the people to prayer, but rather the passing by of the morning's first cattle herd; and, in my terms, half an hour of bartering for a good portrait. Masai clothing is nothing if not vivid, the colour red finding its way into most designs. However, I concluded early in my stay that in order to do justice to the wonderful facial characteristics of the people, the strong colours in their clothes would require to be understated a little. I was not to be disappointed, and several portraits of the women remain amongst my most rewarding work.

Cranes at Roost

Among the leaves

In pensive Mood

The Frown

24

Mother and Baby

2

A brief foray into Islamic Architecture

EGYPT
and TURKEY

Egypt and Turkey

A brief foray into Islamic Architecture

The power and beauty of Islamic architecture have never been in doubt as far as I am concerned. Down the centuries, whether in the context of the Moorish occupation of Spain, the imperial Ottoman presence in Istanbul or, indeed, structural design at its most perfect in the form of Agra's Moghul masterpiece, the Taj Mahal, one variation seems to complement the other. In recognising such beauty wherever it might be, it becomes incumbent on the photographer to do justice to it in its environmental setting, whether this be through a mist, against a sunrise or sunset, or in the bold clarity of urban chaos. Given the choice I must admit that there is little else I would rather do.

It appeared to me that a visit to Cairo and Istanbul in 1992 could offer many opportunities in this regard, and out of deference to its remains of early civilisation, the roots of Christianity and finally the architecture of Islam, my journey to Cairo was eagerly awaited. Situated on the banks of the Nile, it is a great sprawling city with a population of some 20 million people. Given its limited urban boundaries it is arguably the most densely populated place on earth, and from a photographic point of view it both poses problems and provides incentives. In addition to the city's Islamic buildings, its suburban architecture includes structural design from a much earlier age of civilisation, the three great Pyramids of Giza and the magnificent Sphinx. Furthermore, it should not be forgotten that there is a site in Old Cairo where the Holy Family found shelter two thousand years ago when they fled from the wrath of Herod, and Egypt is equally proud of its Christian inheritance, evident in the religious artefacts preserved by the Coptic community.

Because most of my work was designed to fulfil some of the objectives outlined earlier, it was necessary to make visits to Giza in the west and the El Gabal El Abiyad Quarry in the east at dawn or at dusk. Travelling across Cairo by taxi at these times was never going to be easy, and given the stifling heat, the choking dust and the regular problems of directional communication between driver and traveller, excellent opportunities were often missed. Indeed, the possibility of photographing at sunrise had to be abandoned and subsequently all energies were concentrated on Giza and the Quarry at sunset. While the commercial atmosphere at Giza somewhat spoiled a once noble landscape, the eastern elevation of the Mohammad Ali mosque at sunset from the aspect of the Quarry was quite magnificent, even if the Quarry, located near Cairo's military telecommunications headquarters, proved to be a photographer's ambush at the hands of sceptical local military police.

With a little time available before returning to Scotland, it seemed culturally logical to travel home via Constantine's Turkey. The very close proximity of the twin domes of Santa Sophia and the Blue Mosque and their associated minarets presented good opportunities for shooting "into the light". Unfortunately, because of the time of year, to have achieved the correct angle in the early morning, I would have required to have been north-west of the subject, which was not possible because of the topography of the area.

Within the confines of Santa Sophia, once the first great church of Christendom and now an Islamic Museum vending, inter alia, postcards in dubious taste of the Moghul dynasty, certain very important early Christian mosaics are still to be seen. It is fortunate for posterity that when Santa Sophia was overrun by the 13th century Ottomans, these wonderful mosaics were not removed from the church walls but merely plastered over. Restoration work was carried out by Swiss architects in the middle of the 19th century, and in 1932 Thomas Whittemore and other members of the Byzantine Institute began the process of removing the protective plaster covering which had been superimposed.

One of the most beautiful murals, located on the west side of an upper gallery of the church, was uncovered around this time almost in its entirety. I very much wished to photograph this particular mosaic, but a problem of protocol had to be overcome, namely, photographing in Santa Sophia was forbidden. Such a prohibition was not in place out of any religious deference – the sale of tasteless postcards within Santa Sophia revealed little sensitivity or respect for the origins of that particular building – it was more in the nature of a commercial enterprise providing vital income for the city's trade balance.

[Editor's note: the narrative ends at this point, but John Haswell did photograph (presumably when nobody was looking) the mosaic which had impressed him so much, the late 13th-century Deesis Christ, which he used as the subject of his Christmas card in 1992].

Young Egyptian

The Moustache

The Tea Pot

View from the Quarry

The Camel

3

By train though the Bolan Pass

PAK

PAKISTAN

Pakistan

By Train through the Bolan Pass

Most of my journeys were undertaken with due consideration of many differing factors, all relevant to photography. This was not, however, the case when I went to Pakistan. I have a good friend in Edinburgh called Bashir, a fine man and a very proud son of Pakistan. I can recall the many occasions when, head shaking in dismay, he would hear about a forthcoming trip which I was going to make to anywhere, anywhere but Pakistan. It was, therefore, in deference to this friendship that I packed my bags around Easter 1990, heading for a state which is chronologically some 20 days younger than myself.

Geopolitically, Pakistan is divided into four provinces; the Punjab, the North West Frontier, Baluchistan and Sind. In the west, a mountain range forming the border with Afghanistan sweeps down into the fertile plains leading towards their Indian neighbours. My time in Pakistan was shorter than my usual journeys, and because travel and photography were shared with essential visits to kind friends in Rawalpindi, I was unable to visit Lahore, the cultural heart of the nation.

Recalling with schoolboy relish that wonderful yarn of a film, "The North West Frontier", I was particularly interested in travelling by train through the mountains with their passes and gorges between Baluchistan and the North West Frontier Province, and in order to establish a starting point for this journey, a flight to Quetta was necessary. When descending to land at Quetta, the passenger becomes aware of the peculiar design of the town's dwellings – all regular single-storey structures which were built after a devastating earthquake struck the area in 1935, destroying most of the city. I found Quetta a wonderfully friendly outpost, the perfect place for the traveller to establish immediate roots and conveniently situated at the start of the Bolan Pass. This is a railway track running through the Pishin Valley, and on being warned of the likelihood of encountering mountain bandits, the traveller has a genuine feeling of making fearful inroads through robber-infested country. Such negative aspects faded quickly for me, however, as a succession of photo opportunities presented themselves at each station. It was on the journey through the Bolan Pass that one such stopping-place provided the opportunity to photograph a father and son, fellow-travellers, displaying a mixture of diffidence and excitement as they appeared framed in the carriage window. Of the entire portfolio taken on this visit, no photograph gave me greater pleasure.

In the Shade

Seat Taken

Hanging On

Gunsmith

The Face

42

Boy with Spade

44

Confrontation Pendin

The Sentry

4

A rain soaked journey in the land of the Willow Pattern

CHI

CHINA

China

A rain-soaked journey in the land of the Willow Pattern

The moment the first Ming vase, or perhaps an embroidered silk wall hanging, found its way out of China and into the West, the world became aware of something uniquely special, the Chinese landscape. The latitudes and longitudes of China are enormous, crossing some nine time zones between occupied Tibet in the West and Beijing and Shanghai on the Pacific. The nature of the land within its borders is therefore vastly varied. Somewhere, though, in this oriental haystack there must exist a beautiful needle that was so inspirational as to become, across the centuries and many political dynasties, the symbol of the nation; the mountain, the stream and the tree – in short, the elements of the willow pattern. If I was going to take the trouble and incur the not inconsiderable expense, to travel ten thousand kilometres eastwards to an unknown part of the world with photography in mind, my main purpose there would surely be the search for the landscape of that willow pattern now so familiar to the Western World.

My first journey, undertaken in May 1988, was therefore to the southern province of Guangxi, to visit the region of the Li River (Lijiang) between Guangzhou and Guilin. Limestone karsts, formed millions of years ago, provide enormous well-rounded deeply folded mountain scapes, some wooded, others quite bare, one following the other across tens of thousands of square kilometres. There were good reasons for choosing to travel during the early summer, despite the definite risks involved. Rainfall, I was informed, always heavier about that time of the year, creates the most beautiful banks of cloud which float through the river valleys, forming delicately tinted soft cotton-wool buffers between the hard, static karst features, and as the cloud level rises and falls, isolated tree patterns are revealed on the valley slopes. The main risk factor involved was the heavy rainfall, which could not only destroy the delicate balance of nature, but in addition create a danger to life and limb. On reflection, however, I felt that if I were to give myself the best possible chance of experiencing the more positive benefits of that part of the world, the month of May would certainly be the time to make my journey.

I flew to Guangxi Province via Hong Kong and without undue delay checked out the various riverboat journeys available to the traveller around downtown Guilin. Because the Lijiang flows from north-west to south-east, and ultimately into the China Sea at Guangzhou (Canton), the most suitable starting point was Guilin itself. In an attempt to bring to my activities a modicum of self-control, the first river trip was to be undertaken without any recourse to the camera whatsoever. By and large with the exception of recording particular riverside events, the self-imposed control proved successful enough on the first day, and was repeated for confirmation the following day. What I wasn't to know was that the third day in Guilin heralded the beginning of the torrential downpours which were to continue without a break for some six days; so severe were they that half the boat journeys had to be cancelled as the rising water level made the Lijiang the most violent and dangerous of waterways. [Editors' note: It is not at all clear why John put an embargo on his photography during the first two days in Guilin, especially in view of the brevity of his stay and the high risk of heavy rainfall which could occur at any time, and of which he was well aware.]

Desperation was now behind my resolve to board the next of the few remaining boats. Hillside profiles vanished at 200 metres; fisher-men using cormorants, always the most splendid of river features, disappeared completely from view and any chance of settling into a daily river-run, my original intention, proved futile. It was all very well trying to reconcile oneself to the unfolding events by comparing the situation with minor disasters elsewhere: when all was said and done, I had invested a considerable sum of money to get here and produce the goods, and now this possibility was vanishing as fast as the movement of the river currents before my very eyes. I had travelled already twenty thousand kilometres to one of the most beautiful watercourses to be seen anywhere, and now I could hardly see beyond the tip of my own nose. Given such a dispiriting outcome, I was so grateful over the next forty-eight hours to be able to photograph the landbased riverside life between Guilin and Yangshuo, in the shape of a farmer tilling the fields and children playing, their actions caught with a 1000 ASA grade film, in a dark, sombre atmosphere of pea-soup fog consistency.

As if Guilin was not totally satisfied with its evil-eyed warning in the form of diluvial antics, the night before my train journey to Wuhan-on-Yangtze (in search of Humay-Shan, the yellow mountain), the hotel kitchen staff, having lost face over a culinary dispute with me the evening before, contrived to serve up a dish which patently consisted of excessively spiced rice ("let that be a lesson to the likes of you"), and which affected me in the most unspeakable and debilitating form throughout the following thirty six hours. I think any subsequent visits undertaken to Guilin should be covered by some special type of medical insurance.

The Passenger

A Face on the Bus

The Gooseherd

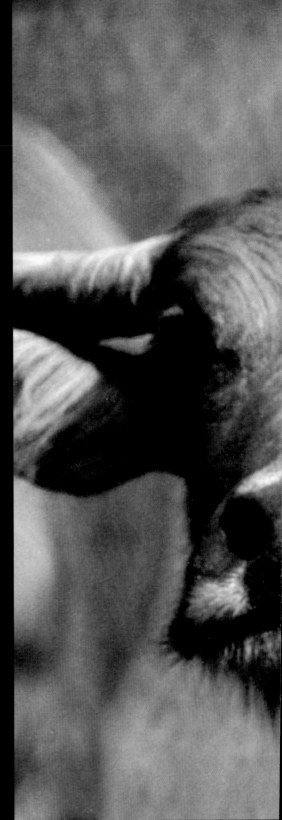

Working Partnership

Tending the Crops

Farm Worker

The Smile

Old Lady with Stick

At the Handlebars

Two Guards

Lunch Time

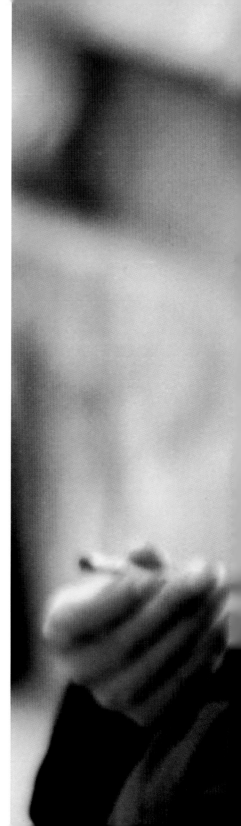

Passing the Time

5

The Mekong Delta -
Bicycles, Boats and Buddhist monks.

VIET

VIETNAM

Images of a Boat Family

The Cyclist

Bike Woman

Three Generations

Young Buddhist Monk

6

A kaleidoscope of unforgettable images

IND

INDIA

India

A kaleidoscope of unforgettable images

In the Spring of 1985 I decided that the first of my adventures with a camera would be to the sub-continent of India. I am not really certain why I chose this direction; I suppose it was not for one single reason but for several, as is often the case. Reading Kipling at an early age probably planted a seed or two, and possibly led me in later life to a closer study of the country and its undoubted attractions; hence I felt comfortable in choosing to explore this vast, complex and visually fascinating part of the world.

India is 83.5% Hindu, the remainder of the people an amalgam of Jain, Sikh, Moslem, Buddhist, Christian and non-believer. To my photographer's mind, the Hindu personality presents itself as open and warm, on the one hand energetically curious, on the other disarmingly shy. They are, in general, anxious to please, and are usually quite disappointed if they consider they have failed in their task. I soon realised that, in photographic and practical terms, such traits would be a distinct advantage during my field visits. Take as an example the young girl, ironing saris in the back street of a shanty-town across the Yamuna from Delhi, revealing the beauty of utter simplicity in the wonderment of finding herself for the first time in her life the focus of a photographer's interest.

The southern Indian states of Tamil-Nadu and Kerala offer lush, verdant hillsides flanking semi-tropical rainforests, which in the case of Kerala in the south-west, are criss-crossed by the Malabar Backwaters, a network of canals providing human and commercial links between hundreds of small communities. Tamil Nadu and its capital Madras are unknown to me, but Kerala I found to be a veritable paradise. St. Thomas the Apostle is reputed to have sailed to Cochin in about 52 A.D., bringing Christianity to this part of India centuries before the arrival of the Portuguese and British colonists. He died a martyr in Madras about 78 A.D. Nowadays, mainly as a result of the Missionary Stations established by the Jesuits in the 16th century, a high standard of education exists in Kerala, so that it is able to export to other states across India its own surplus of the educated.

Far to the north of Kerala and separated from it by seven almost totally Hindu-populated states, lies the equally beautiful state of Kashmir. I was fortunate to travel into Kashmir during my first visit to India in 1985; fortunate because since 1987 the Delhi government has waged a war against the Kashmiri Freedom Fighters and it is at present not possible to travel in this troubled region. Their quest is for a homeland totally free from Delhi and either allied to the neighbouring Moslem state of Pakistan, or autonomous in its own right. A decision was made around the time of the 1947 Partition to keep Kashmir within the national boundaries of India. I cannot recall the reasons submitted for this decision; suffice to assume that when one has such a priceless jewel, retaining possession of it becomes imperative. This action by India is, in a sense, understandable. It is also understandable that the Kashmiris, Himalayan mountain people like their neighbouring Pakistani brothers and, in the main, Moslems, wish to espouse the cause of a cultural and political break from Hindu Delhi. It is indeed sad that Kashmir has now been isolated from the outside world and the would-be traveller to this wonderful area is, of course, the loser.

In geomorphological terms Kashmir is the soft underbelly of the Himalayas; a superb area of mist-shrouded lakes, delicately punctuated by tall, slender willows forming small arbitrary groups or more formally planned avenues, framed by the Karakoram Mountains, the Great Himalayan Range and the Siwalik Mountains. In cultural matters there appears to be little connection between Kashmir and India. However, the easy journey by air to Srinagar from Delhi is only an hour-long flight. On the other hand, the more hazardous land route via Jammu, the gateway to the country, is decidedly challenging but infinitely more rewarding. Cutting across dramatic hard-rock contours, the bus trip provides a two-day mobile balancing act against scree slopes reposing at the most precarious of angles; turbanned hill people, grazing or herding their livestock, stop to glance for a moment as the 1950s Leyland bus labours its way across the tundra or negotiates tightly curving bends around the 1,000-foot screes. Scribbled notes are made en route, proposing a future return to recapture that proud, piercing roadside stare, or that eye-catching cluster of nomadic tents. As sons and grandsons toil on hillsides, the tribal elder statesmen take on, with just as firm a purpose, the tending of the very young. Children returning home from school in some nearby village pose with the confident directness of their Moghul forebears.

If I know little of other Indian states, my experience of Rajasthan is somewhat better. It is the desert state of India, geographically the largest, and yet the least populated. No other Indian state has witnessed so closely the turbulent ebb and flow of political history and survived to tell the tale. As a contrast to the drabness of the arid landscape, the local people love to adorn themselves with brightly coloured clothing, particularly red and yellow.

Each year in November, around the four days of the full moon, Rajasthan devotes itself to a social occasion centred on the small holy town of Pushkar, where, on an open plain to the north, tens of thousands of country folk assemble to create a Fair of overwhelming human colour and energy. Whilst the nearby lake is dedicated to the practice of Hindu religious rites, not too far away more agrarian commerce is transacted during the Pushkar week than at any other single event within the sub-continent. Camels, mainly but not exclusively, are bought and sold in their thousands, along with horses and cattle. At times, across the entire width of the horizon can be seen a colourful assortment of people and animals, the vivid costumes of the former contrasting with the more sober shades of the latter. I was fortunate to be able to travel to Pushkar three times in all, the disappointments encountered on the first visit spurring me on to greater efforts on the two further occasions when I had the privilege of participating in the splendours of this marvellous annual event.

My first visit was marred by the inconvenience of back pain which plagued me during the days before I was due to set off for Pushkar. Kind friends had arranged for a taxi to convey me from Jaipur to Pushkar, a journey which should have taken about half a day. We set off early in the morning at what seemed to me a snail's pace. The driver did not pick up speed when we left the city traffic, as I had vainly hoped, and when I exhorted him to go a little faster he assured me that he would. But he singularly failed to do so, and we arrived in Pushkar at dusk, just in time to see the last camels retreating into the sunset. I vented my frustration on the poor taxi driver, who eventually explained that he had been told by my friends to go very slowly on account of my painful back, so that I would not suffer too many jolts on the unevenly surfaced road. The brief glimpse which I caught of the last vestiges of the glorious spectacle of the Pushkar Fair that day made it absolutely essential for me to return as soon as was humanly possible, to claim my photographic trophies which I knew would be well worth the effort expended, back pain or no back pain!

Fishing Nets near Agra

Gathering Fuel

The End of the Day

amels at Sunset

Ready for the Celebration

The Cyclist

Animals in Perspective

The Hermit

Silhouette at Agra

A Limited View

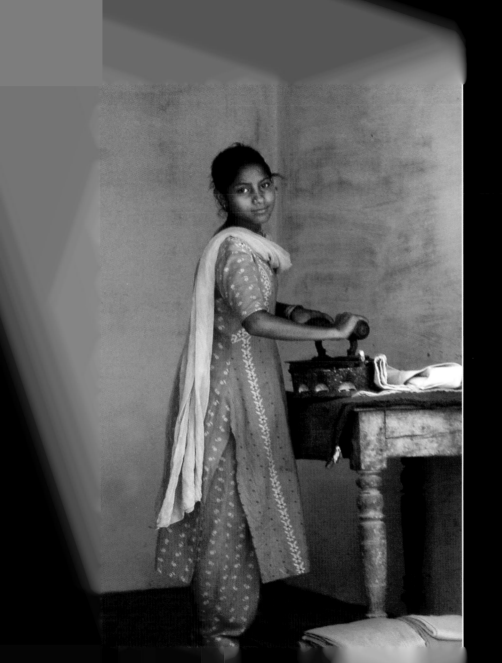

Old beyond her years

Beneath the Veil

Bearded Sage

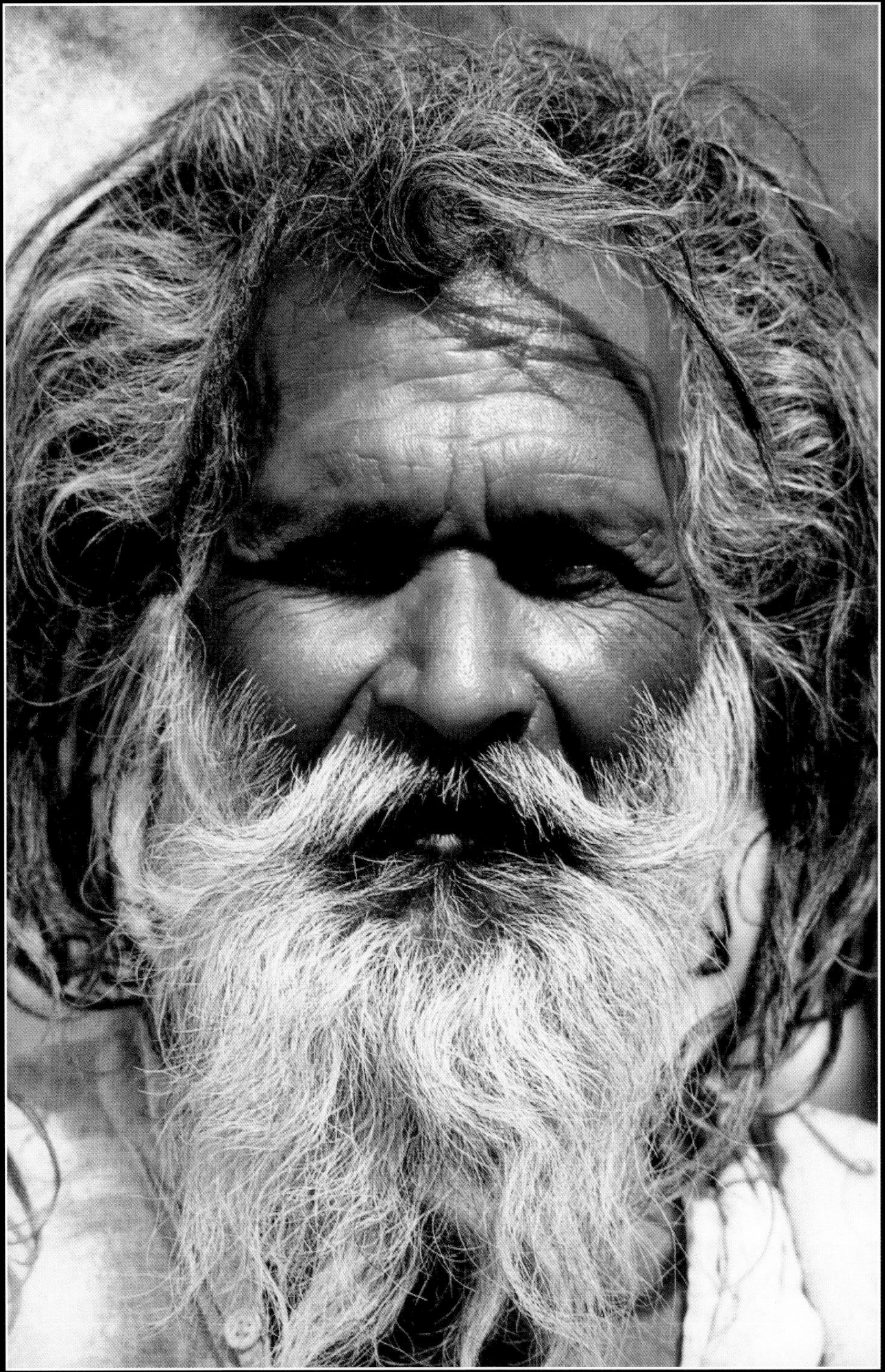

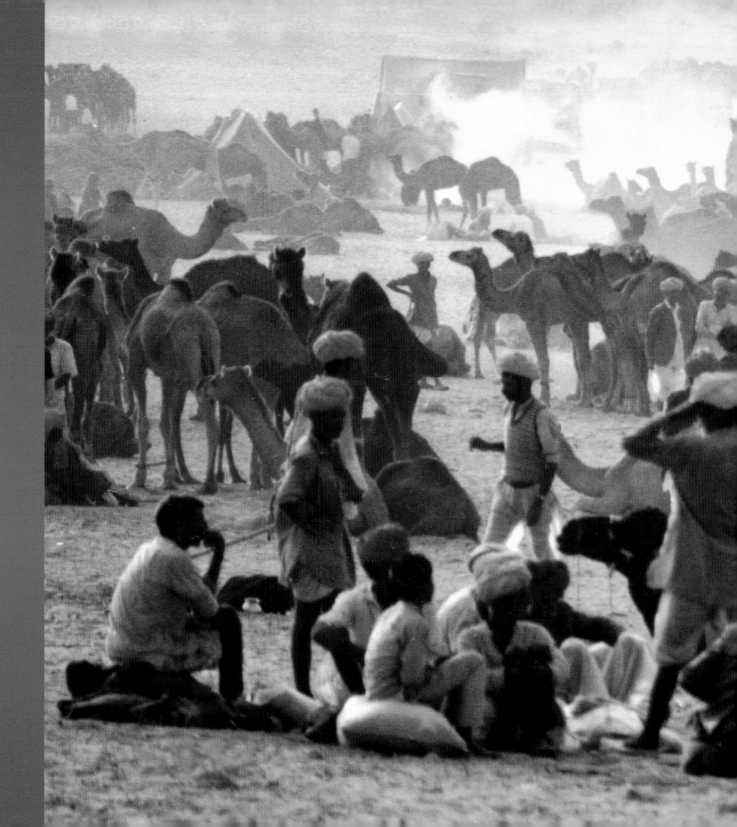

The Camel Fair at Pushkar

Brahma Cattle

The Cattleherd

Images of The Camel Fair at Pushkar

7

Meeting an old friend and making new ones in the land of volcanoes

ECU

ECUADOR

Ecuador

Meeting an old friend and making new ones

I must confess to a strong affinity with Andean South America. Perhaps this comes from early friendships with fellow pupils at school in Dumfries (why and how boys from Chile, Peru and Colombia found their way to the Scottish Borders to be educated I shall never really understand). Or maybe this common bond between Latin America and a child of Latin lineage arose because more Italians than Spaniards – including members of my own family – chose Argentina as a 20th century staging-post. Whatever the reason, when a certain sum of money came my way around Easter 1989 I was on a plane to Ecuador without a second thought.

Ecuador is, in South American terms, a very small country, approximately the size of Wales and situated, as its name indicates, on the Equator. Whilst the country is itself small in scale, topographically it is not. Rising from the Pacific sea-level to an Andean plateau of 4,500 metres' altitude in a relatively short distance, it then drops equally dramatically into Amazonia across the western margins of the Matto Grosso. Its indigenous people are therefore twofold: Andean Inca or Amazonian Indian. As if to reinforce the visual drama of their Andean backbone, with a link from their equally dramatic Inca past, early Ecuadorians named each of a chain of thirteen volcanoes, some extinct, some not, after local gods. Hence, even prior to landing in Quito, the traveller to this country has already flown into and through the "avenue of volcanoes", giving rise to the feeling of having entered a room of Ecuadorian friends, old and new, and shaken the hands of Chimborazo, Cotopaxi and others, before even having landed.

My main purpose in travelling to Ecuador was the photography of local people in their particular environs, either high altiplano or low Matto Grosso. Another objective, however, was to become reacquainted with a local resident who was certainly not Andean. I had first met Father Colin McInnes during a photographic visit to Spain in the late 1960s and had, some years later, sailed in his company through a stormy Sound of Mull in a fragile craft assembled from a DIY kit some days earlier. This experience left me somewhat shaken; not so my companion, who was from sturdy Hebridean stock with an islander's understanding of the sea in all its moods.

Shortly after my arrival in Quito I experienced for myself just how remarkable this man was. My taxi driver had heard of him, but knew little about him. Fortunately a local Italian priest was able to offer directions to El Comité del Pueblo (the People's Committee) – "I don't know where he finds the courage", he confessed, raising his hands to heaven. After some years as a priest in the Diocese of Argyll and the Isles, Father McInnes had made a request to his local Bishop for a parish transfer. If the Bishop had envisaged a straight swap between the Isles, his nephew had other ideas. It appeared that he wanted to be with the poorest of people, living in the most politically unstable of places, and nothing else would satisfy him. And so, this shy, unassuming man had taken on the role of spiritual Pied Piper to some 30,000 souls, long since tired of being the political cannon-fodder of extreme politicians and their henchmen. The barbed wire and flood lights which I saw on my arrival at the church-house of El Comité, San José Obrero (St. Joseph the Worker), indicated that there were forces at play against Father McInnes's parish work. Threats were made on a regular basis by those who did not agree with him that all people are individuals with dignity and should be the slaves of no one. After this memorable visit I made my way to a down-town Quito hotel, and employed the services of César and his battered old automobile. I met César through the Hotel, and over a drink outlined my objectives for the following two weeks. Journeys north along the Pan American Highway to Otavalo or journeys south across the Altiplano to the mid-week country markets; a visit to Amazonia via Ambato, or descending to what he called West-Amazonia for an encounter with the Indians of Santo Domingo de Colorados, were all possible with time, and presumably money. I paid César the equivalent of £17.50 per day, over 10 days. Colin McInnes was to confirm later that such a sum would keep the families of six taxi drivers in grand style for a month or more.

There was no doubt that if portrait photography of local people was to be achieved, then covering the local markets was certainly the way to proceed. I was greatly assisted in meeting these objectives by the fact that all major markets in Ecuador take place up and down the Pan American Highway on different days. Ambato and Latacunga were particularly excellent gatherings. However, I was reliably informed that the Saturday morning fair in Otavalo, a northern town near the Colombian Border, was not to be missed under any circumstances. César and I therefore packed our bags, filled up with cheap diesel and headed for the Pan American Highway. It was a Friday as we slowly made our way through successive Police roadchecks strung across the northern shanties of Quito. It was perhaps no wonder that César was not best pleased when, having made our laborious progress into the countryside and with miles of bad road ahead, I decided on a sequence of roadside stops for ad hoc photography. Because I was reimbursing César on a daily basis, it was difficult to understand his extreme impatience and obvious desire to keep moving. The reason only became apparent after settling into my Otavalo hotel, when I discovered that César, who insisted on staying overnight with "friends" in each town we visited, was in fact driving back home across country to Quito and returning promptly the next morning to resume duties. Any undue delays, therefore, would more than likely upset his hidden agenda.

Disillusioned at César's deceitfulness, I decided the best way of forgetting my annoyance was to go out and explore the town's old Spanish Colonial Square, already beginning to fill with early arrivals for Saturday's prompt 5 a.m. start. Now, in hindsight, I cannot thank César enough for his gestures of disloyalty. Having decided to think positively, I fell by chance on a situation that was to yield the most productive single hour's photography of my life so far. In struggling to overcome the twin obstacles of poor and fading light and the unhappy husband of an Otavalo Indian wife, herself very pleased to be photographed, I was nearly on the point of giving up, when I became aware of a child standing behind me, quite absorbed in the fruitless goings on. An Otavalo Indian girl, she had forsaken her traditional attire for a Western appearance, the mandatory Andean felt hat being the only exception. A dedicated portrait photographer never fails to seize the opportunity when a genuinely interesting face presents itself, and having won her confidence, I was able to take a series of delightful studies.

Otavalo Indian G

High Style

Prepared for the worst

Benign Old Age

110

Free Ride

En route to the fair, Otavalo

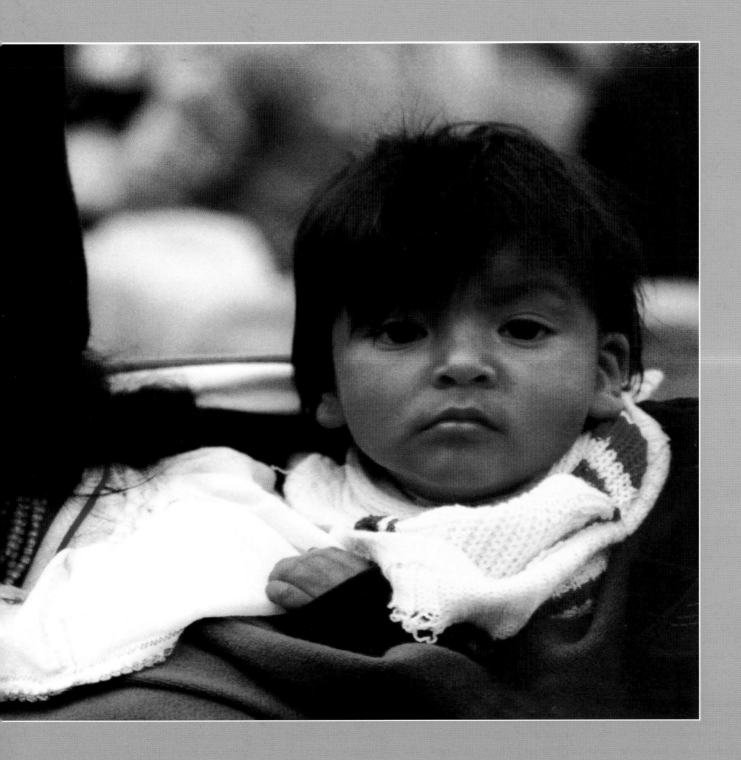

A short winter visit to Moscow

RUS

RUSSIA

Russia

A short winter visit to Moscow

As Autumn turned to Winter towards the end of 1989, the prospect of travel deep into Eastern Europe was not a particularly attractive one. How fascinating after all would it be to photograph the faces of a nation protecting itself against the annual threat of frost bite? Equally, most species of indigenous flora and fauna would by now be well and truly into hibernation. In addition, on the few occasions of photographic mechanical failure I had experienced in taking some 25,000 photographs, low temperature conditions were never entirely innocent by-standers.

So what was behind such an unusual change in direction? Well, I suppose the main trigger that prompted a visit to Moscow in late January 1990 was a single vision created by a fellow photographer. A number of years earlier I had been shown a photograph of such compelling beauty that it became in my own mind's eye an object lesson in the art of photographic composition. The location was Moscow's Red Square; the vista, south towards St. Basil's cathedral taken from high up on the Museum of National History; and most importantly, the time – Winter – with its powerful low-angle cross-shadows.

The gauntlet, therefore, was thrown down more quickly than the disappearance of mid-Winter's setting sun. My flight fare from London, so I was assured, was a partly subsidised one, courtesy of ITV Sports wishing to commandeer most of the aircraft for the purpose of covering the European Ice-Skating Championships in St. Petersburg (then, of course, called Leningrad). Armed with this assurance from my fellow travellers, I was quite happy to assist them in the capacity of technical-apparatus-carrying donkey on arrival at Sheremetyevo Airport.

Having acquired before I left home most of the preliminary knowledge required for successful photography of the striking Byzantine architecture which awaited me, I had felt quite comfortable on the ride from Sheremetyevo Airport to Central Moscow, until the diabolical thought crossed my mind, "You are here for a mere four days; what on earth made you think that in the Winter of a godless nation like Communist Russia, the Almighty would grant you four days of unbroken sunlight?!" I had this unsettling thought just as my bus passed into Revolution Square, behind Red Square, and ground to a halt in half a metre of snow – which certainly had not arrived in Moscow courtesy of the Sun-Gods. Moments later, we were to be enveloped in the first of many snow-storms that would recur at fairly regular half-hour intervals during that long, cold, white week-end.

I had done some research in Edinburgh on the location of my chosen subjects prior to leaving for Moscow, and my first task was to find the most sensible method of travelling to the Novodevichy Convent. Taking into account my utter incomprehension of the language and the fairly limited time available for each project, there seemed only one possible method of transportation for me – the taxi. That decision having been made, I stood on the Kalanin Prospekt repeating to myself over and over again in pidgin Russian the basic instructions which I would need to give to the driver. A taxi pulled up, my carefully rehearsed phrases were delivered, and we were on our way.

The Novodevichy Convent, tucked into a bend of the Moskva River, is an impressive complex of buildings within massive crenellated fortress walls, incorporating a cluster of gilded pepper pot domes belonging to the 16th century cathedral, a spire-crowned portal and an interesting old cemetery containing the tombs of many illustrious Russian cultural and historical figures. In bygone centuries Russian architects loved to adorn their most significant buildings, and whenever they contrasted sombre colours with gilded domes, spires and other features, the result is sublime. So, sitting in the taxi, with dreams about to come true, my Winter dash to the land of the Urals seemed justified. Life again was good and it looked as if he who strove would soon be rewarded. It was as simple as that.

Simple, until the realisation dawned that we were on the Komsomolskiy Prospekt, parallel to the Moskva River and heading fast through the rapidly disintegrating slush, in what appeared to be the wrong direction. Sudden panic was assuaged by the conclusion that the driver had lived in Moscow a lifetime, myself a mere lunchtime. Any moment now, I thought, the cold watery sun would surely be in the right part of the sky – but ten minutes later the position of its quickly disappearing image still did not give me any reassurance. Novodevichy was obviously a place which had to be approached by stealth, in a subtle and devious manner.

I had not been in Moscow long enough to witness any shades of Russian emotion – but the display by Ivan my taxi driver, who was on a fixed fee, made Nikita Kruschov's tantrums at the United Nations seem positively low key. It is at times like these – and I must confess too many for comfort – that the end product, the photograph, soothes the soul. And so, the arrival at my film-set combined with my departure from Ivan (who was given a 20% tip) was adequate compensation for the morning's travails. Here, pepper-pot angles were established, portal-spire perspectives noted and 19th century double-glazed reflections achieved. The acquaintance of a courtyard artist was also made; I was grateful for this because, with the arrival of late afternoon, temperatures fell dramatically – and this kind soul, stationed at his easel like a block of ice for apparently most of the day, shared with me the dregs of his thick soup and a portion of stale bread. Then young Valery, arriving from nowhere, took an interest in what I was doing, asked a thousand questions and received not a single answer, nevertheless offering to transport my spare gear on his winter-sledge. Our group increased to four with the arrival of James, a political journalist from Washington D.C. – "just sight-seeing, I guess, just killing time, that's all" ... He was in Moscow to cover the mini-Summit due to be held in the following week.

Whether or not James and I were particularly inclined, the twelve year old Valery firmly declared that we could not leave Novodevichy without visiting the famous cemetery next door, not always open to tourists. This worried me a little. James, I felt, was too laid-back for political journalism. Could he be at the site for darker, more sinister reasons? Somehow, idle chatter around the precincts of Novodovichy was fine, but wandering about with a child and a spy in a frozen Russian graveyard introduced an element of danger. After all, John Le Carré and Graham Greene had taught us all, long ago, how the innocent are caught up with the guilty. It was, therefore, with a certain amount of anxiety on my part that three people, complete strangers only 15 minutes before, explored together this fascinating place of the dead. In a strange way it was also alive, but only with the names of some of Russia's greatest personalities who were resting there – writers, musicians, painters and statesmen – the only creatures capable of understanding the running commentary of a young Russian boy, anxious to please visitors to his country. Among them was Rimsky-Korsakov, whose music I had much admired as a young man, loving the energy of his Capriccio Espagnol; and Nikita Kruschov, in Soviet terms anonymously laid to rest beneath black and white marble to signify a checkered past.

Our sojourn amongst the famous in fact passed pleasantly and uneventfully and in time, as the winter daylight quickly faded, I parted company from my fellow travellers without being arrested as an accomplice in the trading of State Secrets. Such relative success always arrives with a price to pay; in my case, I had very few photographs to show for my first full day in the Soviet Union, and 25% of my time lost. My return to Novodevichy the following day was unquestionably to correct that situation; to atone for my slothful ways I also attended an Eastern Orthodox Service, and later in the day gazed at Comrade Lenin, resting peacefully in his three-piece pinstripe below the Kremlin Wall. I do hope, I recall thinking, that they don't bury me like that; I could be taken for an arch capitalist.

Sun and Snow in Red
Square

St. Basil's Cathedral, Moscow

Late Afternoon Shadow at the Convent

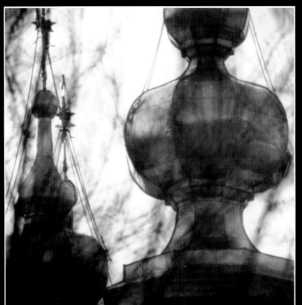

Convent Detail

Golden Domes

A Symphony of Domes

Young Valery

The Autumn of Life

123

The Novodevichy Convent

9

Bonding with the Berbers
and travelling with the Tuaregs

MOR

MOROCCO
and ALGERIA

Morocco and Algeria

Bonding with the Berbers and travelling with the Tuaregs

The chain of Mediterranean countries spread across North Africa appear like a family of nations, representing Arab brothers of broadly similar lifestyles existing under a variety of Islamic standpoints, some fundamental, others not so. From a geographical point of view this part of the world, stretching from the shores of the Atlantic in the west to deep into Arabia in the east, is to a large extent an endless land-mass of flat desert. As if to protect all fronts east of it from the force of the Atlantic Ocean, a range of mountains has been thrown up into sharp relief, and it was in order to explore the terraces of the Atlas Range and meet the people indigenous to these parts, the Berbers, that I chose to join a truckful of travellers in the summer of 1989. My interest in this region was initially awakened by a painting I had come across years before, depicting all the basic elements of the Atlas and its Berber inhabitants; the foreground being a high, wide plain traversed by djellaba-clad locals either mounted or on foot, travelling between scattered villages of square, mud-walled dwellings clustered or individual, and interspersed by dark green oases of fig trees and date palms, with the snow-capped High Atlas Mountains beyond.

The imperial cities of Fez and Marrakech, whilst important in a cultural sense, were not vital for my purpose. There is never much beauty in urban chaos, however historical the setting, and I found much more of worth in Morocco's high plateaux, deep gorges, oases, villages, and to the east and south, its Saharan margins; and what provided a further dimension, its people. The Berbers are a colourful, friendly and intelligent race, always ready to share their time and mint tea with visitors to their country. A good example of their legendary hospitality is shown by the fact that it was to the ancient city of Fez that the Jews came, after their expulsion from Spain in the 15th century, remaining there for hundreds of years and continuing to live in perfect harmony with their Berber hosts.

In the quite enchanting fortified Kasbah of Air Benhaddon I was fortunate to meet a family that reflected the very best of Berber hospitality extended spontaneously to the complete stranger. Walking along a hot, dusty back street in half shade, I observed from some distance an elderly person, sitting alone in front of her home, dreaming dreams, no doubt, across a Berber lifetime. Expecting the usual reaction of the older, more traditional female citizen of that part of the world, I was surprised to be greeted not only with genuine curiosity but, even more endearingly, with a warmth of hospitality. The fact that we could not converse did not appear to concern her too much, and when a young man appeared who could speak English, she assumed the rôle of the third party with resignation. Explaining to the new arrival the reasons for my stay in Air Benhaddon and requesting obliquely where I might photograph some of the locals, I was surrounded by his sisters, equally friendly and, as I recall, all very beautiful. Strangely enough, despite the obvious attraction of the sisters, I felt compelled to concentrate my efforts upon the old lady sitting in front of the house.

Travelling west through the lovely Draa Valley on a hot and dusty morning, I came into the fortress town of Ouarzazate with its interesting Kasbah. Mindful that one is more likely to gain relief from the heat by taking an even hotter drink, I went in search of a café – always an excellent vantage point from which to observe the local scene – and it was there that I met a date farmer from a nearby village. This man was well known, mainly because of losing his immediate family as a result of a car crash on the road between Marrakech and Ouarzazate some years earlier, from which he himself escaped without serious injury. I saw him the following day and found that he was in a sense a newcomer to the area, his forefathers having come from near Merzonga on the edges of Moroccan Sahara. Our common language was pidgin French, and after walking the length and breadth of his date farm with him, I was able to secure a portrait of this sad man bereft of his family, the useful life in him now appearing irrelevant to his present lonely situation.

During my trip to Morocco in 1989, I chanced to find lodgings in Marrakech's Hotel de Foucauld, a rambling old watering hole of French Colonial design, located just behind the city square. This was my first "encounter" with someone who was to inspire my visit to the Algerian Sahara. Since he actually died in 1916, I am obliged to use the word "encounter" in the loosest of ways. Again, perhaps the word "died" conjures up in the mind the gentle passing away of just another of life's citizens. In the case of Charles de Foucauld, this was certainly not so. Father de Foucauld died a most violent death, his throat cut by a single thrust of a sharp Tuareg knife, wielded by someone who unfortunately was not aware of the good work which the priest had been doing among their tribe. The bloody deed was perpetrated in the red-brown fort which he had constructed in the Saharan Tuareg capital of Tamanrasset to protect the inhabitants from marauders. Devoted to understanding and befriending the Muslim Tuareg people, and where possible to building bridges of trust between the peoples of Islam and Christianity, he tried to establish common parameters between these two great religions. He was ordained a priest in 1901 and immediately began his charitable work among the desert dwellers. In 1910 he was responsible for the building of hermitages and chapels in Tamanrasset and some 80 miles further north on the edge of the Assekrem Plateau in the rugged and fascinating mountain area of the Hoggar. Mass is still said in the little chapel attached to the hermitage, where relics of Father de Foucauld can be seen. The hermitage and chapel are tended nowadays by the Petits Frères de Jésus, founded in 1933 and inspired by the life and work of Charles de Foucauld.

My quest for further knowledge of this remarkable man, who prior to his conversion had in early manhood plunged deeply into the fleshpots of late 19th century France, had established that from the vantage point of his Hoggar chapel, some 300 metres above the hermitage, Charles de Foucauld witnessed a vision each morning at sunrise, so magnificent and powerful that he judged it to be no less than a daily visit from the Almighty. I was becoming more and more intrigued, and by late November 1991 a return ticket to Algiers had been obtained. As is normal during the mechanics of organising any trip, there was the usual haggling over money and time off work. The Director of my firm offered me no more than the equivalent of a single week's leave. Would it really be possible to travel to the Central Sahara, traverse the Hoggar, find the

129

hermitage at Assekrem and record de Foucauld's vision all within that short space of time? I thought it was most unlikely, indeed almost impossible. However, despite being turned away at London Heathrow for lack of a suitable Visa and thus losing two precious days, and also suffering a bout of altitude sickness in the Hoggar, the results of this brief trip remain extremely satisfying.

I travelled via Algiers to Djanet, an oasis town of the Tuareg and former outpost of the French Foreign Legion. The Algerian Sahara is so enormous that the flight within this barren country took longer than the first leg from the United Kingdom. I remembered prior to landing on the sand-covered tarmac strip, the warning that Djanet was just as important for military purposes as it was for Tuareg local colour and as such, taking photographs around the landing strip was strictly forbidden. It soon appeared that a crucial decision had to be made – a good photograph or a spell in jail. If it turned out to be the latter, then so be it. As I descended the open stairs of the Boeing 737 on to the Djanet landing strip the first opportunity for a photograph materialised before me – four six-feet tall Tuaregs fraternally embracing each other, their flowing indigo robes aglow in the scorching sunlight – going to jail for this stolen moment was, therefore, not so difficult an option. And indeed I did go to jail, but only for three hours or so. Rescued by my local travel agent (minus photograph), I was released into the old town square, where I had a rendezvous to keep with Osman, the Tuareg "Prince", a man proud to the point of arrogance, but commanding a lot of influence in the area. It was therefore vital not to lose his good will. The days I spent with Osman and his three guides took us and our 17-strong caravan on an almost circular route north-west of Dgault, through hard-rock gorges cut through some of the most spectacular formations ever yielded by the earth's crust, across vast flat plains of coarse gravels, and over never-ending waves of dunes, shaped by the wind into fluid architecture.

Viewed closely, the camel offers few attractions. The Tuareg blue-clad men of the desert obviously turn a blind eye to the physical imperfections of this thoroughly odd-shaped, cantankerous, spitting and biting animal because of its immense value as a beast of burden with an unrivalled ability to travel long distances over desert terrain without replenishment of food or water. I was, however, very much aware that a camel caravan travelling across vast desert expanses shaped by the wind provides limitless photographic opportunities, animals and nature combining in perfect visual harmony. Early nightfall saw our ships of the desert tired and listless, front legs now hobbled, dispersed to the four quarters of the compass, to be retrieved with unfathomable efficiency some twelve hours later from wherever their wanderings had led them, spit-stained Tuareg attire only hinting at the struggle required to subjugate them for yet another day's work. To help them cope adequately with their harsh surroundings, nature has moulded the Tuareg into a hard, fit, uncompromising creature, tall and slim as a reed. Although maintaining a proud dignity, they are quite approachable and are happy to regale visitors with their excellent mimicry and colourful stories of past adventures.

Father de Foucauld's vision in the Hoggar was finally captured by my camera for eternity on the last day of November 1991, the feast of St. Andrew, as the priest reminded me after Mass when he enjoyed the luxury of a piece of my shortbread, the 'Biscuit Ecossais' as he called it. John Major was Britain's new Prime Minister, confirmed by an aged Tuareg riding past on a camel and much to my surprised amusement shouting "Majeur! Majeur!" at regular intervals.

At the Well

Oasis Man

Camels

Desert Caravan

The Date Farmer

Tuareg Blue

Friendly Old Lady

Protected from the Elements

The Goatherd

The Defile

Moonlit Ridge

Sahara Moonscape

Hard Going

10

Images of Venice, its people, and the Carnival.

ITA

ITALY

Gondolas at Rest

Reflections

Waiting for Customers

The Voyeur

The Onlooker

Study in Gold

Prickly

Well Composed

Overlooked

Making a Point

Scarlet Lady

Deep Purple

Man and Mask

The Blue Headscarf

The Gold Mask

Unmasked

The Tear

The Lagoon at Sunset

Impressions of the Lagoon, Venice

Triptych in Red

Reflections of
San Giorgio, Venice

The Blue Veil

The Scottish Casket:
John Haswell's final journey

EPILOGUE EPILOGUE

EPILOGUE

Epilogue

The Scottish Casket:
John Haswell's Final Journey

In my brother's Will he requested that his ashes be taken to the Benedictine Abbey at Monte Cassino in southern Italy and cast to the four winds. Our maternal grandparents had come from a small hilltown some twelve miles from Cassino, and I therefore recognised the request as an understandable wish on John's part to return to his roots.

At his funeral in Edinburgh some months earlier, I had been the victim of an unfortunate typing error. As I flicked through the parish bulletin the evening before John's funeral Mass, I noticed with much knee-trembling the announcement of my own death and funeral, not John's. It is at moments like these that you wish you could phone a friend, or go 50/50 with the Almighty. In accepting the weakness of my position, I recalled a family history of sibling rivalry and silly pranks, conceded defeat and awarded John the winner's medal for black comedy. I somehow imagined that John had played his trump card and that all other bets were off. Little did I realise what else he had planned!

British Airways, when approached about the delicate matter of taking ashes abroad, said they could do the business, and advised me to bring enough evidence to convince Her Majesty's Customs and Excise of the sincerity of my mission. Forewarned of the intended plan, the Scottish funeral directors constructed a special casket for the ashes, coffinesque with brass nameplate, and capable of withstanding the pressure of high altitude flying. It was heavy and somewhat macabre, justifying, for practicality and privacy, the acquisition of a special canvas carrier. I have often gulped at the emotion engendered by this ghoulish container. I then remind myself that it was manufactured in Edinburgh. Could one really have expected less from the city which gave us Burke and Hare? Armed with the casket, death certificate and John's passport, I set off for Heathrow, prepared to prove that I was not smuggling cocaine. A luggage scanner was employed to test the casket for foreign objects in a very polite procedure which, nevertheless, caused some consternation to onlookers. When asked if I minded this examination, I reasoned that as John had been through the rigours of the crematorium he was unlikely to object to the X-rays of Heathrow; and in any case he had always had a healthy interest in photography. The British Airways chief steward announced that he was expecting 'us' and introduced me to his personal locker, behind the cockpit, where he placed the casket, stating sincerely, "We don't want any accidents in the overhead locker, do we?"

Within 10 minutes of take-off I was approached in my Economy Class seat by the steward, who then discreetly asked me to come forward to accept an upgrade to Business Class. It wasn't just a seat he offered me: it was a complete row. I was impressed by the attention, but I was not prepared for what followed. "Help yourself to the champagne, sir, while I get your brother for you." He returned with the casket, placing it on the adjoining seat! When he took my order for lunch, I was fully expecting him to offer a double whisky "for the wee man in the box"! In fact, before landing, he returned to present me with a large bag full of alcoholic miniatures, announcing that British Airways wished me a pleasant onward journey and a good night's sleep! The strange experience was completed with my arrival in Rome carrying two bags – one containing alcohol, the other the ashes of my brother – who detested flying but tolerated the experience with the help of a drink or two. It all began to make surreal sense.

By now I was becoming familiar with the plurality of my position. This was not my mission to Monte Cassino – it was John's final journey. Like so many of the incident packed camping trips we had undertaken as teenagers, we were in this together. Accordingly, the reader will not be surprised to learn that the casket accompanied me for supper to a little restaurant off the Piazza Navona, and to Sunday Mass the following morning. The Piazza was one of John's favourite photographic haunts and I am sure he would have approved of the choice for our Last Supper.

My overnight hotel was half way between the Vatican and the Termini Stazione, well placed for a short 10-minute bus journey to the rail station – or so I thought. With initially well over an hour to spare, I queued in vain for a space on the No. 64 autobus, failing in three attempts to get on board the packed vehicles. With 20 minutes to spare, I finally found myself in transit, tightly sandwiched between tourists and locals. I did not feel the hand which removed my wallet as I clung to my precious cargo and watched the remaining minutes tick away. I was in the station queuing for the ticket to Cassino when I first felt the emptiness of my pocket. I had been robbed, and I descended into dark fury and deep panic. It is at moments like these that you realise why adrenaline is brown. There were seven minutes remaining before the departure of the Cassino train. The next one, some two hours later, would have been too late for my planned visit to the monastery, and there were friends waiting for me in Cassino. Their details had been in the wallet along with my Italian money and cheque cards.

To the astonishment of travellers on Platform One, I unpacked the casket, revealing a hidden store of sterling beneath the ashes. In our early travels together the habit had been to split the resources, thus minimising the risk of complete disaster. This journey was no exception. Following a quick dash to the cambio and a short phone call home with instructions to cancel all stolen cheque cards, I was back in the ticket queue. There was clearly no time to report the theft. When I subsequently did so, the Rome police correctly predicted with almost smug satisfaction that it was the No. 64 bus – this apparently being the epicentre for pickpockets in the Eternal City. It was no consolation to be told that detectives regularly travelled this route.

I was greeted in Cassino by Italian family friends from the north east of England, Agnese Geldard and her brother Ciro. Her family, as ours had formerly been, was locally based and she was nominated in John's Will to be there in Monte Cassino on the appointed day. I shared the drama of the previous hours with them over a relaxing and necessary glass of Frascati, before we commenced the long climb up to the monastery in Ciro's car. The locals were enjoying the early evening sunshine and promenading in the central rose garden in large numbers as we arrived. Others were admiring the view from the public balcony. Together they presented unexpected obstacles to the completion of our mission for they occupied the natural locations for disposal of the ashes. There is a classic prisoner of war film called "The Wooden Horse" in which prisoners disposed of excavated material by gradual deposition down the trouser leg into the topsoil of the parade ground. This option was only briefly considered! There being no obvious alternatives, we decided to present our dilemma straightforwardly to the monks and seek access to a private location within the monastery.

The English-speaking receptionist, a graduate, was sympathetic and put our case to the monk on duty. His response however, was negative and emphatic. I attempted to gain some credibility and support by proving a local link through reference to my great uncle, Padre Angelo Coia, a young priest who served the town until his death in 1916, and is now buried in land adjoining the monastery. But this was to no avail. It soon became clear that the practice of cremation was not fully accepted in Italy, and certainly not yet by the Benedictines. In translating the message of rejection, the receptionist privately hinted that if we returned five minutes before closure she would do what she could to help.

Returning at the appointed time, we were greeted by the receptionist and proceeded to the now deserted rose garden. Two of the monks suddenly came forward from the adjoining cloister, barring our way with their presence, using raised voices and forceful language. They had been in waiting, clearly anticipating our return. The unpleasant scene was embarrassing for all concerned, ending emotionally with tears shared by the ladies present. Clearly the receptionist had risked her job to help us. In tears she concluded in strained English that "It would have been easier if you had brought the body". Whilst the embarrassment of being discovered was matched by the emotion of argument, both were eclipsed by the realisation of impending and inevitable failure. We retreated in silence to the public car park.

What happened next is the stuff which restores one's faith in the Almighty and mankind. As we approached our car, the solitary remaining vehicle in the car park, another came into view. It had a punctured front tyre and belonged to the head gardener. Deciding not to risk leaving his vehicle overnight in the public car park, he opened the gates into the monks' private garden, of which he was the custodian, to repark his beloved Fiat. We followed, quickly explained our dilemma, and received the supportive approval of the gardener. John's ashes were sprinkled around the base of a solitary tree in the serenity of the monastic garden; he looks west into warm Italian sunsets and rests peacefully and privately in the garden of those who would not have him.

On returning to my hotel later that evening, we were greeted by the friendly receptionist from the monastery and her boyfriend. She had trawled the hotels of Cassino to apologise for our harsh treatment by the monks and to offer other solutions to our dilemma. They joined us in our private celebration of a mission accomplished, and shared a few bottles of Frascati. It was the end of an emotional day. I had been robbed in Rome and 'monked' in Monte Cassino. My sleep that night was well earned, but short lived.

My wake-up call came not from Reception but from my friend Ciro, back home in his village, with the warning of a one-day rail strike, effective from 9 a.m. that very morning. There was no time for a shower or shave. Within five minutes I was outside the hotel waiting for a taxi, desperate to catch a train heading north from Cassino before 9 o'clock. I was 80 miles from Rome and there remained 6 hours to catch the return flight home. As the taxi jerked to an abrupt halt, the passenger door opened, almost as a gesture of Italian hospitality. I had accepted the lift before I realised that the self-opening door was not really a special welcoming feature but the product of poor design or lack of maintenance in the locking department.

Worse still, the driver seemed totally ignorant of this basic weakness in his offer of transport. A brief visit to the stazione proved that the strike was already in force. Hundreds of frustrated Italians looked around for a second Mussolini to get the trains back on schedule before bartering over the few taxi deals on offer. At least I had one, and a driver who was willing to take me to Formia, a small coastal town through which, he assured me, the Napoli-Milano express would be running – despite the national strike. I explained that I had no Italian money and accepted his offer.

Inside nearly every Italian male is an undiscovered Formula One hero, and every taxi driver believes that his Fiat is really a Ferrari. The acceptance of these self-evident truths is crucial to the understanding of the journey that was to follow. The driver prepared for take-off by closing all the car windows and seeking permission to smoke – "to calm his nerves", or so he declared. For my part, I became uncomfortably conscious of the loose door and decided to thread my seat belt through the door handle before securing it to the central stanchion. My driver grinned in support of this innovation, clearly believing that it had brought added value to his would-be Ferrari. The entire journey was undertaken at great speed, with much overtaking and little braking, in the classic Formula One tradition. The horn was used regularly and as the principal protection for overtaking on blind bends. My requirement to catch this train was the justification for a whole range of illegal manoeuvres and would no doubt have been his justification to the carabinieri, should they have been capable of catching us. Sharp intakes of nicotine appeared to coincide with high points in acceleration or crossing double white lines.

The white-knuckle ride from Hell ended peacefully in anticlimax, as I disengaged myself from the tension of the taxi's cockpit in a side street in Formia. I had expected quite reasonably to be taken directly to the stazione; instead I found myself outside the Banco di Napoli. The driver's cunning plan now became obvious. Knowing that I had only English currency, the journey had been undertaken at extra speed to allow me to visit the bank! The experience cost me almost £80. Those who can recall my brother's tales of unforgettable taxi rides will see the parallel theme in my own experience.

The strike-breaking express from Napoli stopped at Formia as promised, and I successfully joined the stampede of locals in climbing aboard, and stood for the journey to Rome. The scene on arrival at Termini Stazione was complete chaos. The metro which provided the link to the airport was also a victim of the national strike. With no time to queue for the autobus, I spent £35 on another expensive and exciting taxi ride to the airport.

My stolen wallet had contained the voucher for my car in the long-stay car park at Heathrow. I spent twenty minutes in the rain finding my car and almost twice that time attempting to prove to Heathrow staff that I had only been away for three days – not three weeks. In desperation I produced the Scottish casket, told a shortened version of this story, and watched the opposition disappear in a mixture of shock and embarrassment. I am sure there was much laughter in Heaven at my expense. Furthermore, I cannot recommend this experience to anyone – but I have a useful tip to pass on. If you want to fly in total comfort, take a box of ashes and do the obvious – travel with British Airways.

David Haswell

The Abbey at Monte Cassino: Journey's End

GAVENNY GRAPHICS